501 Excuses To Go Golfing

will golf 4 food!

Justin J. Exner

© 2001 Justin J. Exner

ISBN: 0-9665319-9-X

Library of Congress Number: 00-107658

Illustrations and Layout by Dawn M. Emerson

Edited by Gayle Breunig

Visit us on the web at www.501excuses.com

Published in 2000 by
Greenleaf Book Group LLC in Cleveland, Ohio

2000 First Edition, First Printing

First and foremost, I want to thank God, not only for the ability to golf, but the family and friends he has blessed me with.

I dedicate this book to my entire family, with special thanks to my father Terry, my mother Janet, my sister Jayne, and my brother Jason. I love you all.

In addition, I would like to thank Dawn Emerson and Clint Greenleaf for all their hard work.

Please support your local charities.
It does make a difference.

Justin Exner earned a B.A. in Aviation Business from Embry Riddle Aeronautical University in Daytona Beach FL. In 1998, he received his MBA from Franklin University in Columbus, OH. He spends most of his free time traveling and hunting for little white balls in forests. Justin currently resides in Northeast Ohio.

You should never need an excuse to go golfing, but...

1.

I had to drive all the way to another city to help you move, I'm sure going to golf.

. . . .

2.

The doctor said after getting an injection, I must keep my arms loose.   Golfing is the best thing.

. . . .

3.

With the economy doing so well, I need to take up a new expensive sport.

. . . .

4.

The weather has been so bad lately, I want to take advantage of the sunny weather.

. . . .

5.

I finished all my projects at work.

. . . .

6.

Since winning the Lottery, I need something to occupy my time.

. . . .

7.

My father's will stated I had to spend the money on green fees!

. . . .

8.

Winter is coming. I need to get out as much as possible.

. . . .

9.

I was motivated by play on the US Open.

. . . .

10.

I have to get used to my new putter.

. . . .

11.

I received a new sleeve of balls for my birthday.

. . . .

12.

My wife is due with our first child. I have to play as
much as possible before he is born.

. . . .

13.

I really need some form of exercise.

. . . .

14.

I have been working way too hard; I need to relax.

. . . .

15.

The storm knocked out the electricity, so the office is
closed.

. . . .

16.

The IS department won't be able to fix the server till
next Monday, so we are taking the week off.

. . . .

17.

The doctor recommended I golf every day. . . I think
that's what he said.

. . . .

18.

You are not allowed to wear a tie on the golf course.

. . . .

19.

It's the only thing I can do at 5:30 AM.

. . . .

20.

The courses are too busy on weekends, so I am
going out today.

. . . .

21.

The lawn mower is broken.

. . . .

22.

My wife went to a baby shower and I have nothing to do.

. . . .

23.

My girlfriend went out with her friends.

. . . .

24.

The wind may help me reach the par-5's in two.

. . . .

25.

I think I can win closest to the pin
in the charity golf outing.

. . . .

26.

It's Father's Day; I'll do what I feel like.

. . . .

27.

It's a requirement at the next sales meeting.

. . . .

28.

I need to get a better tan.   It's never cloudy on a golf course.

. . . .

29.

I got a gift certificate for a free round of golf for my birthday.

. . . .

30.

It's half price green fees before noon.

. . . .

31.

The British Open has me all excited.

. . . .

32.

I am almost 50; I need to practice for the senior circuit,

. . . .

33.

There is beautiful swan watching on the fairways.

. . . .

34.

It's the perfect place to get together and discuss life with co-workers.

. . . .

35.

I enjoy nature.

. . . .

36.

My wife bought me new clubs for my birthday.

. . . .

37.

I heard a new tee box was added.

. . . .

38.

I heard a new sand trap was added to #4.

. . . .

39.

My e-mail is down at the office.

. . . .

40.

The junkyard didn't have the part I needed, but it was
next to a course I haven't played in years.

. . . .

41.

My son was suspended from school, so I thought I'd take him golfing as punishment.

42.

My brother-in-law has a layover on his way east, so I thought we could catch up while playing nine.

. . . .

43.

I can expense it for business purposes.

. . . .

44.

I have a few hours to kill before the M*A*S*H reruns start.

. . . .

45.

I wasn't able to golf in the outing last week, so I'll go today.

. . . .

46.

I collect used tees in all the tee boxes.

. . . .

47.

I don't have time for the driving range, but I have time to play 18.

. . . .

48.

I always meet interesting people on the course.

. . . .

49.

The golf course is the only place I get good customer service.

. . . .

50.

The grass is too wet to cut, so I might as well just go golfing.

. . . .

51.

It was such a long winter, this spring weather makes me feel like golfing.

. . . .

52.

I need to teach my son how to drive.
The golf cart is the perfect instructional tool.

. . . .

53.

My girlfriend went to the movies,
and I need to kill a few hours.

. . . .

54.

I haven't played the course in ten years
since I moved away.

. . . .

55.

The union at work furloughed me,
so now I have free time.

. . . .

56.

My wife took lessons, so now
I have to take her out on the course.

. . . .

57.

It's raining, and I need to see if my new rain gear is effective.

. . . .

58.

There are excellent fairway bunkers on this course.

. . . .

59.

I have to teach my son-in-law how to golf.

. . . .

60.

There is an opportunity to see OJ on the course.

. . . .

61.

I got a super deal on a golf package.

. . . .

62.

I have never had the chance to golf in Arizona.

. . . .

63.

They say the greens are tough in Myrtle.   I have to try
it for myself.

. . . .

64.

My wife wants to have sex, so I'm going golfing.

. . . .

65.

The course is allowing me to demo clubs for free today.

. . . .

66.

I got my new handicap card and want to show the guys
at the club.

. . . .

67.

I lost my keys on the course last year, and I'm going to keep playing until I find them.

68.

What else am I supposed to do on vacation—spend time with the kids?

. . . .

69.

I have never eagled a hole before.   I feel lucky.

. . . .

70.

The clubs are the only things I got in the divorce settlement.

. . . .

71.

It's the first day above 50 degrees.

. . . .

72.

They are offering 18 holes for the price of 9.

. . . .

73.

The fish are not biting this time of year.

. . . .

74.

The bowling alley was closed.

. . . .

75.

I can shoot par on the computer version now I want to try the real thing.

. . . .

76.

The Cubs missed the playoffs, so my afternoons are free.

. . . .

77.

I got a new beer coolie.   I have to try it out on the course.

. . . .

78.

Someone asked!

79.

I could finally afford a pair of name brand clubs—I want to see if I can break 120!

. . . .

80.

I had back surgery yesterday.   I need to see if it helped!

. . . .

81.

I went to the ballet last night, so my wife is letting me go golfing today.

. . . .

82.

It's the only place I know where I can get a free pencil.

. . . .

83.

I have to try my new sand wedge.

. . . .

84.

I can get some lawn care tips from
the ground maintenance crew.

. . . .

85.

They have a great microbrewery at the clubhouse.

. . . .

86.

They put in a nursery at the clubhouse, so I can have
them baby-sit and me golf!

. . . .

87.

I heard they cut the greens again.   I have to try them
out.

. . . .

88.

I have to try out this new hat.

. . . .

89.

I got a new pair of knickers.

. . . .

90.

Last time I was out, I had a hole in one. I couldn't
finish the round because I was so excited.

. . . .

91.

They have really soft toilet paper at the golf course.

. . . .

92.

The course serves a great club sandwich for lunch.

. . . .

93.

My wife is having a baby shower at our house.

. . . .

94.

The sun is shining.

. . . .

95.

My wife is making me teach her how to golf.

. . . .

96.

My house is being painted. I need to get out for a
couple of hours.

. . . .

97.

My car is being fixed, again!

. . . .

98.

My kids are away at camp.

. . . .

99.

My wife was yelling at me, so I had to get out of the house.

. . . .

100.

I have to see if these new golf balls will float.

. . . .

101.

It is a three-day weekend and my wife has to work.

. . . .

102.

I enjoy looking for my ball in the rough.

. . . .

103.

It's the only fun thing I can do with my family.

. . . .

104.

I'm locked out of the house and I only have keys to the car trunk (where my clubs are).

. . . .

105.

I just got new glasses; I have to see if I can follow the ball.

. . . .

106.

It's the first day of spring; I might as well go golfing.

. . . .

107.

I have to test this new allergy medicine—the course is the perfect testing ground.

. . . .

108.

The movers are packing my house. I have nothing else to do.

. . . .

109.

I missed the shuttle bus, so I can't go to work.

. . . .

110.

I have never played a canyon course before.

. . . .

111.

I'm trying to conserve energy, and the course uses electric carts.

. . . .

112.

I got lost going to work and ended up at the golf course.

. . . .

113.

I was their one-millionth golfer and I was given a year's worth of greens fees.

. . . .

114.

My doctor instructed me to take up a non-stressful sport!

. . . .

115.

I have to see if I eliminated my slice.

. . . .

116.

I've been practicing at the range every day.   I need to see how I will do with a real course.

. . . .

117.

My dad always pays when we go.

. . . .

118.

I work nights; I have nothing else to do during the day.

. . . .

119.

I'm home shopping, and my real estate agent is taking me golfing to show me a few houses.

. . . .

120.

I have to golf as much as possible.   Here in Alaska we can only golf 4 months out of the year.

. . . .

121.

I hate Nascar, and that's all that's on TV.

. . . .

122.

My dog ran away and he always goes to the golf course.

. . . .

123.

The rough is real playable on the course.

. . . .

124.

All the pin placements are forward today.

. . . .

125.

My tires are being changed.   I need to kill a couple of hours.

. . . .

126.

It's an absolutely beautiful day; they can't possibly need me at work.

. . . .

127.

They don't make you rake the traps at this course.

. . . .

128.

It's league play day.

. . . .

129.

Summer is almost over, and I just have not played enough.

. . . .

130.

They put new tee boxes on the par-5's.

. . . .

131.

I have not played since last summer.

. . . .

132.

I need to break in my new golf shoes.

. . . .

133.

My sister asked me to take her.

. . . .

134.
My wife is making me go!

. . . .

135.
Tomorrow is ladies day, so I have to get out today.

. . . .

136.
My golf pro said I have to go at least once a day.

. . . .

137.
I am sick of playing golf on my computer. I want to play for real.

. . . .

138.
I got those new golf balls that fly "too far"; I have to try them out.

. . . .

139.

The driving range is closed, so I have to practice somewhere.

. . . .

140.

I just got an 87-degree wedge that if swung properly, will go backwards.

. . . .

141.

Senior citizens get a discount this year!

. . . .

142.

I sprayed my balls with silicon, which guarantees my ball won't slice.

. . . .

143.

I bought those new golf contact lenses, guaranteed to cut 5 strokes off your score.

. . . .

144.

My doctor told me to walk as much as possible.   I might as well walk from the cart to my ball!

. . . .

145.

I need practice; the Masters is on TV next week.

. . . .

146.

The weather forecast next month is for rain; I need to get in as much golf as possible.

. . . .

147.

I like the beer girl, so I have to play every day in order to talk with her.

. . . .

148.

I read somewhere golf is good for the back.

. . . .

149.

I need some peace and quiet.

. . . .

150.

I am required to golf for work; I love my job.

. . . .

151.

The phone lines are down at work.

. . . .

152.

I have been taking golf vitamins, which are supposed to allow me to hit the ball an extra 10 yards.

. . . .

153.

Why not go golfing?

. . . .

154.

I need to get out on the course before it snows any
more.

. . . .

155.

They didn't promote me at work, so I am taking as
much time off as possible.

. . . .

156.

My game is starting to come together, and I need to
keep sharp.

. . . .

157.

My kids keep want and try to beat me.

. . . .

158.

I lost all the skins last week; I need to try and
win the money back.

. . . .

159.
My boss wants me to play in a scramble.

. . . .

160.
My son was sick, and I have to fill in as the fourth.

. . . .

161.
The course just opened.

. . . .

162.
Last week I almost broke 100.   I have to keep trying.

. . . .

163.
What else would I do on vacation?

. . . .

164.

I have been practicing putting on my carpet; now I want to see if the practice has paid off.

165.

I like taking the perfect divot.

. . . .

166.

I couldn't golf when I was married, so any time is good now.

. . . .

167.

I have to pay the country club dues, I might as well get my money out of it.

. . . .

168.

The practice area has a sand trap.

. . . .

169.

The weather is beautiful.

. . . .

170.

Because I am retired.

. . . .

171.

I have a rain check from yesterday.

. . . .

172.

I have to practice for the tournament next week.

. . . .

173.

My wife said if I cleaned the garage out, I could go; so I took my clubs out of the garage and put them in my trunk and went golfing.

. . . .

174.

I have to keep trying to get a hole in one!

. . . .

175.

I called in sick at work.

. . . .

176.

The course has a special before 7:00 AM.

. . . .

177.

The leaves are changing colors.

. . . .

178.

I need to play 20 times to get my handicap established.

. . . .

179.

I get more work done on the course than at the office.

. . . .

180.
My flight canceled, so I need to kill a few hours.

. . . .

181.
My wife took the kids on vacation.

. . . .

182.
I got the membership as a gift for Christmas.

. . . .

183.
I won a new set of clubs; I no longer have to rent clubs.

. . . .

184.
I need to try my new spikeless shoes.

. . . .

185.

I woke up in the parking lot of the golf course.

186.

I have to take my wife golfing at least once a year; it was in the prenuptial.

. . . .

187.

My wife cut me off, so I have to get rid of my physical exertion.

. . . .

188.

I watched the pros on TV, and it looks easy, so I want to try it.

. . . .

189.

I golf around Chicago, hoping to see Michael Jordan.

. . . .

190.

There are a lot of cool frogs near the ponds.

. . . .

191.

My grandfather taught me to golf and I want to keep his legacy going.

. . . .

192.

The golf course is where I write my books.

. . . .

193.

They have the best driving range.

. . . .

194.

I golf at the outings, hoping to win the car.

. . . .

195.

I want to become a
professional golfer, so I need the practice.

. . . .

196.

I enjoy driving the golf carts.

. . . .

197.

I bought a whole new golf wardrobe.

. . . .

198.

There is nothing like a long, slow walk in nature, with no one in front of me.

. . . .

199.

I read it was good aerobic exercise.

. . . .

200.

I liked playing in the sand as a child; I simply continue to enjoy it as an adult (kind of).

. . . .

201.

It is rumored they lowered the cost of beer at the course.

202.

My friend keeps telling me it's fun.

. . . .

203.

I bought a golf cart at a rummage sale.

. . . .

204.

It gets me out of the house.

. . . .

205.

Golf teaches me patience, and I need a lesson.

. . . .

206.

I enjoy hitting things.

. . . .

207.

My buddy is the starter, and he sneaks me on the course for free.

. . . .

208.

My wife went furniture shopping

. . . .

209.

We are having the family reunion at the golf course.

. . . .

210.

I heard golf is much easier when you're sober, so I have to try it.

. . . .

211.

My wife is out shopping for curtains.

. . . .

212.

I'm so late for work, I'm just not even going to go in.

. . . .

213.

I have a meeting at the course, so I might as well go golfing.

. . . .

214.

The ATM made a mistake; now I have some extra money.

. . . .

215.

They give out free peanuts at the turn.

. . . .

216.

The forecast is for snow; we need to play as much as possible today.

. . . .

217.

I only need eleven more rounds to establish my handicap.

. . . .

218.

It is the first day all week it has not rained.

. . . .

219.

I finished cutting my grass.

. . . .

220.

I just received my unemployment check.

. . . .

221.

I just bought my new car; I need to see if it will make it all the way to the course.

. . . .

222.

It's easier than doing my taxes.

. . . .

223.

The doctor said running is bad, but walking with golf clubs is OK.

. . . .

224.

My back hurts, so I'm going golfing.

. . . .

225.

The course does not require you to replace divots.

. . . .

226.

The pool is closed, so I'm going golfing.

. . . .

227.

I need to find more golf balls, and it's the best place to look.

228.

My hose is broken so I can't wash the car; I might as well go golfing.

. . . .

229.

It's the perfect way to get to know my future father-in-law.

. . . .

230.

My wife is driving me nuts, so I'm going golfing.

. . . .

231.

I need to lose some weight; it's the perfect exercise.

. . . .

232.

It's my wedding anniversary, so I'm going golfing.

. . . .

233.

My motorcycle broke down right in front of my favorite course.

. . . .

234.

My son turned two yesterday. I need to practice, so I can show him how to play.

. . . .

235.

I got kicked out of G.A. (Golfers Anonymous).

. . . .

236.

I like playing scrambles.

. . . .

237.

My college roommate is in town, and it's the only thing we have in common.

. . . .

238.

My company sponsored an event, and I was asked to play.

. . . .

239.

I need some more excuses for bad golf shots-I am writing a book!

. . . .

240.

I want to show off my new sand wedge.

. . . .

241.

I have to make sure my back stays loose.

. . . .

242.

I just love to golf.

. . . .

243.

My girlfriend asked me to get out of the house for a few hours.

. . . .

244.

I have to see how my new lesson worked out.

. . . .

245.

I took the day off because my office is being painted.

. . . .

246.

I really just like the scenery on the golf course.

. . . .

247.

I got the hots for the beer girl.

. . . .

248.

I enjoy the peace and quiet on the course.

. . . .

249.

My new socks are supposed to fit in my golf shoes better.

. . . .

250.

There is nothing else to do in northern Wisconsin.

. . . .

251.

I lost too many balls playing tennis; I want to try golf!

. . . .

252.

My wife is taking the kids golfing. I think I'll tag along.

. . . .

253.

My horse is sick, so polo is out of the question for today.

. . . .

254.

All the cool kids play golf.

. . . .

255.

I like watching the geese on the course.

. . . .

256.

I have a scramble next week. I need the practice.

. . . .

257.

I gambled away my mortgage money last week, so I need to win it back today.

. . . .

258.

I am just very optimistic I will play well if I golf today,
so I'm going!

. . . .

259.

My new golf shorts have a special built-in pocket to
hold tees.

. . . .

260.

It is better than cleaning out the garage.

. . . .

261.

My broker offered to take me.

. . . .

262.

The clubhouse was just remodeled.

. . . .

263.

The greenskeeper just planted new flowers.

. . . .

264.

I just finished taking a lesson on the Internet; I want to see if I improved.

. . . .

265.

It's Augusta!

. . . .

266.

I golf every day that ends in a "Y".

. . . .

267.

It's the only thing to do in Las Vegas.

. . . .

268.

My father asked me to teach him, again!

. . . .

269.

The doctor ordered me to get lots of fresh air.

. . . .

270.

I kept missing the balls playing softball.

. . . .

271.

The smoke looks so cool on the pond in front of the
first tee box.

. . . .

272.

My back is finally feeling better.

. . . .

273.

The golf course serves the best canned beer in the city.

274.

Who needs an excuse to go golfing?

. . . .

275.

I need to see if my clubs will fit into the
trunk of the new car.

. . . .

276.

It feels great fixing ball marks on the green.

. . . .

277.

I have some extra money for greens fees from my
company's profit sharing.

. . . .

278.

I do all my praying on the course.

. . . .

279.

I just like wearing golf shoes; they are so comfortable.

. . . .

280.

I support my family by selling the golf balls I find
in the woods.

. . . .

281.

I like going swimming in the clubhouse pool after I golf.

. . . .

282.

History indicates the more I play, the better I get.

. . . .

283.

My best friend is taking me golfing for my
bachelor party.

. . . .

284.

I've only played 12 rounds this week; I need lucky 13.

. . . .

285.

I never regret going golfing.

. . . .

286.

It's where the taxi dropped me off.

. . . .

287.

I've never golfed in Scotland.

. . . .

288.

I love the way the sun rises on the fairway.

. . . .

289.

I came home from work, and a note instructed me to leave and go golfing.

. . . .

290.

I want to try out my new lob wedge.

. . . .

291.

I learned a new putting technique, which makes me only one-putt.

. . . .

292.

I need to try my newly regripped clubs.

. . . .

293.

That's where they told me to go for the job interview.

. . . .

294.

I was physically forced to join the company's golf league.

. . . .

295.

I have to golf; it's a guy thing.

. . . .

296.

It's an opportunity to play a course I have never played before.

. . . .

297.

You get a free lunch with every round of golf.

. . . .

298.

I had a dream last night telling me to go golfing.

. . . .

299.

I just play well when the wind blows out of the north.

. . . .

300.

I have spent a lot of time practicing; I want to see how
I do.

. . . .

301.

I have a coupon from the newspaper.

. . . .

302.

It's a habit.

. . . .

303.

They put in a new sand trap on the long par-5 fairway.

. . . .

304.
They clean my clubs after the round is over.

. . . .

305.
Standing over a birdie putt is just thrilling.

. . . .

306.
I had to make a sales call at the course anyway.

. . . .

307.
It is an opportunity to meet new friends.

. . . .

308.
I need to try my new carry bag.

. . . .

309.

I bought a double
titanium krypton driver
with atomic shaft and
sand grooved grips.
I need to try it out.

310.

They gave me free greens fees because it was so slow last week.

. . . .

311.

I can finally keep my driver in the fairway.

. . . .

312.

I want to see if my new ball retriever works.

. . . .

313.

I heard the course is flat—I always play well on flat courses.

. . . .

314.

It's the only sport I can take up at age 60.

. . . .

315.

I need to work on my slice.

. . . .

316.

I sponsored a hole at the charity event.

. . . .

317.

It's the first day of the summer.

. . . .

318.

I'm happiest on the golf course.

. . . .

319.

It was my mom's suggestion.

. . . .

320.

I have an opportunity to play with the three best players at the club.

. . . .

321.

I had new soft-spikes put on my golf shoes.

. . . .

322.

I always play well when it rains.

. . . .

323.

I won greens fees in the employee raffle.

. . . .

324.

I have to see if my new sunglasses really help me read the greens better.

. . . .

325.

I have already seen all the movies at the video store,
so I'm going golfing.

. . . .

326.

I just got tungsten irons in the mail.

. . . .

327.

I don't have a logo ball from that course.

. . . .

328.

I have only played that course on my computer.

. . . .

329.

I just love teeing it high and letting it fly.

. . . .

330.

I think I can finally beat my wife.

331.

My cell phone is out of range at that course, so my boss can't reach me.

. . . .

332.

My mom is taking the kids to the amusement park— so I'm taking the afternoon off.

. . . .

333.

My house is being remodeled, so I need to get out of the house.

. . . .

334.

The course has great drinking water at the tee boxes.

. . . .

335.

The fairways are like greens, and the greens are like velvet.   I just have to play it.

. . . .

336.

I really like a good challenge; golf is the only sport that humbles my ego.

. . . .

337.

If you buy a dozen golf balls at the pro shop on Tuesdays, they will let you stay and play.

. . . .

338.

It's a holiday; what else should I do?

. . . .

339.

When you buy 18 holes, you get the second 18 for free.

. . . .

340.

The clouds are just white and puffy.   Perfect golf clouds.

. . . .

341.

The wind is blowing out of the south; I may be able to par the number one handicap hole.

. . . .

342.

It's rained a lot lately.   My long irons will stick the green.

. . . .

343.

I lost my work ID, so I might as well go golfing.

. . . .

344.

I quit smoking, and a golf course provides a lot of fresh air.

. . . .

345.

I gave up intimacy with my wife, so this is my new vice.

. . . .

346.

My softball game was snowed out, so I might as well go golfing.

. . . .

347.

I had a sunroof put in on my golf cart. I need to try it out.

. . . .

348.

They are fumigating my office, so I have to find something to do this afternoon.

. . . .

349.

I was laid off, so I might as well go golfing.

. . . .

350.

My wife made me join her golf league, so we can spend quality time together.

. . . .

351.

The Cub's have a night game, so I might as well golf this afternoon.

. . . .

352.

My girlfriend bought me a perspiration-free golf shirt.

. . . .

353.

They are having an open house on my home, so I have to find something to do.

. . . .

354.

I just can get more business done on the course.

. . . .

355.

They are giving away free golf tees with every nine holes purchased.

. . . .

356.

I like the feeling of the wind blowing in my hair when I drive the golf cart.

. . . .

357.

All the executives from my company play this course.

. . . .

358.

The course has the best Philly cheese steaks at the turn.

. . . .

359.

I had to join the course so my wife could make some friends.

. . . .

360.

A free round of golf was included with lessons.

. . . .

361.

I may be able to play by myself.   I always score better!

. . . .

362.

My next door neighbor asked if I wanted to go.

. . . .

363.

It's the only challenge I find
(besides talking with my wife).

. . . .

364.

There is a traffic jam, so I might as well play nine
instead of sitting in traffic.

. . . .

365.

The course just put in new golf ball washers.

. . . .

366.

The voices in my head told me to go golfing.

367.
I enjoy the smell of freshly cut grass.

. . . .

368.
I just returned from Antarctica. I am really craving the frustration of playing bad golf.

. . . .

369.
All the TV shows are reruns.

. . . .

370.
Replays are only $20.

. . . .

371.
My mom is making me teach my little brother to golf.

. . . .

372.

I just finished the book titled "Learn to Golf in Twenty Minutes".

. . . .

373.

They installed rain guards on the back of the carts to keep my clubs dry.

. . . .

374.

I like playing cards in the locker room when I'm done golfing.

. . . .

375.

My wife has custody of the kids for the next two weeks, so I have plenty of free time.

. . . .

376.

My new towel is supposed to clean my clubs with one swipe.

. . . .

377.

We lost electricity in our house.

. . . .

378.

The sky is the perfect shade of blue.

. . . .

379.

I got new license plates for my golf cart today.   I want to see how they look.

. . . .

380.

I lost my driver's license and the closest place to walk is the golf course.

. . . .

381.

Monday Night Football moved back to 9:00 p.m., so I have the entire evening.

. . . .

382.

I can pass gas, and no one is the wiser.

. . . .

383.

Church was canceled because of all the snow, so I'm going golfing.

. . . .

384.

I just love to golf new courses.

. . . .

385.

This course has the best sand traps.

. . . .

386.

When I visit my brother, that's all he does, so I have to golf.

. . . .

387.

The bachelor party starts on the golf course.

. . . .

388.

My girlfriend's grandma cooks such good meals; the course is the only place to walk off the meal.

. . . .

389.

I like the break of the greens on this course.

. . . .

390.

I finally can make my ball go left to right.

. . . .

391.

I have been taking anger counseling for my golf game.

. . . .

392.

I almost broke 90 last time out.   I need to keep
trying.

. . . .

393.

I have never played bent grass before.

. . . .

394.

The course put in a new irrigation system on the back
nine.

. . . .

395.

The yardage has all been remarked.

. . . .

396.

I love long par-5's over ponds.

. . . .

397.

The golf course is the only place I can get my entire family together.

. . . .

398.

Golf brings out my best competitive nature.

. . . .

399.

The creek is dried up, so I won't lose a ball on my approach shot.

. . . .

400.

I have never birdied a #1 handicap hole.

. . . .

401.

I just bought a pair of waterproof shoes with the slip-proof soft-spikes.

. . . .

402.

The course is trying out a new program with water coolers on all the carts.

. . . .

403.

I just had graphite shafts put on my clubs.

. . . .

404.

I like to think about life while I golf.

. . . .

405.

This new course has valet parking.

. . . .

406.

I just bought a box of titanium golf balls.

. . . .

407.

Golf fills the long void of the weekend until work starts again.

. . . .

408.

My wife looks sexy carrying golf clubs.

. . . .

409.

Golf is the only place I can take my girlfriend where she can't talk constantly.

. . . .

410.

I started to follow through on my swing.

. . . .

411.

I just bought a new golf glove off the web.

. . . .

412.

Those new thin tees allow me to hit my drive an extra 10 yards.

. . . .

413.

I received a demo package of the liquid core golf balls.

. . . .

414.

I learn from the other player's swing.

. . . .

415.

I finally have a chance to play with someone worse than me.

. . . .

416.

I enjoy looking through the used golf balls in the pro shop.

. . . .

417.

I enjoy wearing golf caps.

. . . .

418.

The course has great golf magazines in the bathroom stalls.

. . . .

419.

Since getting my new camera, I collect photos of every green.

. . . .

420.

The course we are scheduled to play has a lot of hills.

. . . .

421.

I just turned 65; I can now play the gold tees.

. . . .

422.

I love the decision-making part of golfing.

. . . .

423.

I heard they got rid of the port-o-potty at the turn.   I have to crown the new bathroom.

. . . .

424.

I just bought a putter that is guaranteed to cut 10 strokes off my round.

. . . .

425.

I have been watching the golf channel for 48 hours straight.   I am psyched to try what I learned.

. . . .

426.

My carpet at home just doesn't break like a real green.

. . . .

427.

I can finally play under pressure, so I can start betting
again.

. . . .

428.

I like playing with these guys; they don't make me putt
out.

. . . .

429.

You can get the best cigars on the golf course.

. . . .

430.

The new rakes for traps are supposed to allow the ball
to fly out of the sand easier.

. . . .

431.

The humidity is low, so I won't sweat.

. . . .

432.

Drinking beer and golfing is just fun.

. . . .

433.

I just got a new yardage gauge.

. . . .

434.

I have been on a plane all day; I just really need some
fresh air.

. . . .

435.

We might play a links course; I wouldn't have to see
any other golfers.

. . . .

436.

I need to try and fish my driver out of the pond.
I left it there last time I played.

. . . .

437.

My new golf bag has a cooler that guarantees beer to
stay cold for five hours.

. . . .

438.

I like collecting yardage books.

. . . .

439.

My wife lets me golf, if I go to church.

. . . .

440.

My new shoelaces are guaranteed to lower my score.

. . . .

441.

I like seeing my footprints on the dew in the early morning.

. . . .

442.

I just enjoy having a cup of coffee while waiting on the tee box each morning.

. . . .

443.

They just replaced the rye with bluegrass in the fairways.

. . . .

444.

I have to pick up a club I left at the course yesterday.

. . . .

445.

I just bought some slice-proof tees.

. . . .

446.

I played so bad last week; I just want to get back out.

. . . .

447.

My wife only lets me play miniature golf; I need the real thing.

. . . .

448.

I want to play in Denver; the ball flies farther.

. . . .

449.

I like using the ball washers.

. . . .

450.

Frustration is a rush. I can only get that on a golf course.

. . . .

451.

I get depressed when I don't play.

. . . .

452.

I just learned how to hit the ball left to right. I think I can finally control the ball.

. . . .

453.

When the course is dried out, I can hit the ball a lot further.

. . . .

454.

I'm getting married this afternoon. I need to sneak in 36.

. . . .

455.

I just want to play an entire round without a shank.

. . . .

456.

I prayed I would shoot even par.

. . . .

457.

I usually play real strong on the nineteenth hole.

. . . .

458.

I slowed down my back swing. Now I need to see if it helps my game.

. . . .

459.

The course just installed electric ball washers.

. . . .

460.

I just won the slice-free driver.

. . . .

461.
This course offers free caddies with each round purchased.

. . . .

462.
I like saving score cards from every round I play.

. . . .

463.
The course guarantees no flies or mosquitoes.

. . . .

464.
My wife is pregnant, and she just wants me out of the house.

. . . .

465.
They just got all new range balls.

. . . .

466.

After reading the USGA rules, I have to change my theory on golf.

. . . .

467.

I just bought winter golf gloves.   I want to see how they work.

. . . .

468.

Free beer at the turn.

. . . .

469.

The superintendent just replaced all the sand in the traps.

. . . .

470.

I just got the high spin, titanium-tungsten-liquid filled golf balls.

. . . .

471.

I like golfing because I can pee outside.

. . . .

472.

The rain has blown through, and the sun is shining.

. . . .

473.

I missed my flight because security was backed up, so
I might as well go golfing.

. . . .

474.

My psychiatrist hypnotized me, and I am guaranteed
to shoot par.

. . . .

475.

I just love screaming the word "Fore".

. . . .

476.

It's the only place I know where
women won't bother me.

. . . .

477.

My chiropractor has cracked my back, allowing
me to extend my follow-through.

. . . .

478.

With the wind blowing, I can drive
the greens on the par-4's.

. . . .

479.

My wife bought me a pair of those golf undergarments.

. . . .

480.

The softball game was rained out.

. . . .

481.

I'm hungry, and a hot dog just tastes better on the course.

482.

I am useless at work unless I golf twice a week.

. . . .

483.

I like the benches at the tee boxes.

. . . .

484.

My wife went shopping and asked me
not to be home when she returns.

. . . .

485.

They are offering a free round of golf with
a nights stay at this hotel; I'm considering
moving in permanently.

. . . .

486.

My team didn't make the play-offs; now I'm off in the
afternoons.

. . . .

487.

I want to try that new glow-in-the-dark golf.

. . . .

488.

The wind is blowing.

. . . .

489.

A free round of golf was thrown in for test driving the car.

. . . .

490.

The course is going to aerate the greens next week.

. . . .

491.

I was late for my job interview, so I might as well go golfing.

. . . .

492.

My wife is busy washing the dog. I think I can sneak out the back door.

. . . .

493.

My wife went house hunting with her sister.

. . . .

494.

My grandma instructed me to go.

. . . .

495.

I'm hopelessly addicted to golfing.

. . . .

496.

I like seeing the fish in the ponds when I look for my ball.

. . . .

497.

I just rarely get the opportunity to play that course.

. . . .

498.

It's the perfect place to teach my son anger control.

. . . .

499.

The speed of play on this course is excellent.

. . . .

500.

I like reading long putts.

. . . .

501.

Excuse? I don't need no stinking excuse!

What is your favorite
excuse to go golfing?

You can send your best excuses to us
via our website at
www.501excuses.com

If you provide us with an original excuse
that we use in our next book, we'll
send you a free copy.

Look for Justin's other book:

501 Excuses for a Bad Golf Shot

Available at local & internet bookstores.

Wanna make a bulk purchase
of Justin's books for your golf
outing or for corporate gifts?

Contact us at
(800) 932-5420
or email us at:

sales@greenleafbookgroup.com

Order additional copies of this book as gifts for your family and friends!

Call toll-free (800) 932-5420

or

Send us your name, address and phone number, with a check for $10 per book payable to Golf Excuses, LLC to:

Golf Excuses, LLC
P.O. Box 811252
Cleveland, OH 44181-1252

or order at
www.501excuses.com

*For information on
freelance artistry by
Dawn M. Emerson please
call (216) 224-GOLF or*

*e-mail
dawn@greenleafbookgroup.com*

For information on publishing a book of your own, please call Greenleaf Enterprises, Inc. at (800) 932-5420.